Table of Contents

 with CD

ISBN-13: 978-1-61928-030-4

THE FJH MUSIC COMPANY INC.
Frank J. Hackinson

Production: Frank J. Hackinson
Production Coordinators: Joyce Loke and Satish Bhakta
Editors: Joyce Loke, Edwin McLean, and Peggy Gallagher
Art Direction: Andi Whitmer – in collaboration with Helen Marlais
Cover Illustration: ©2012 Susan Hellard/Arena
Interior Illustrations: ©2010 Susan Hellard/Arena
                      ©2012 Teresa Robertson/Arena
Cover and Interior Illustration Concepts: Helen Marlais
Engraving: Tempo Music Press, Inc.
Printer: Tempo Music Press, Inc.

CD 2 • MIDI 1

Technique at the Piano

1. **Warm-up**
Stand tall and well balanced. Roll your shoulders three times slowly forward and then three times slowly backward. Then slowly move your head to the right and then to the left. Repeat all three steps.

2. **Review of triads and inversions**

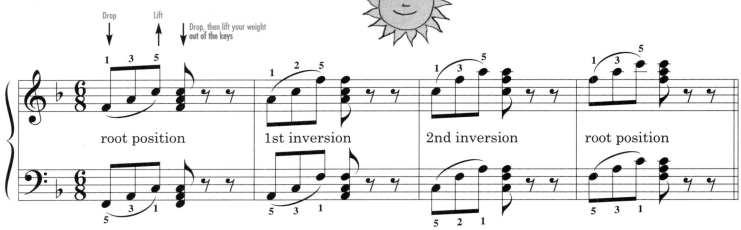

Play L.H. one octave higher if you like!

3. **Root Position and 1st inversion triads**

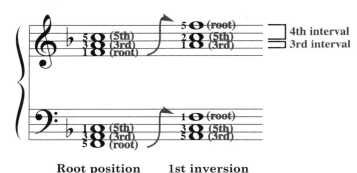

Root position   1st inversion

- When the **bottom** note is moved to the top, it is called an inversion.

- Play these triads and remember the fingering.

4. Write the fingering below for F Major and D Major. Then play. Try playing them with your eyes closed to remember the shape of the chords on the keys.

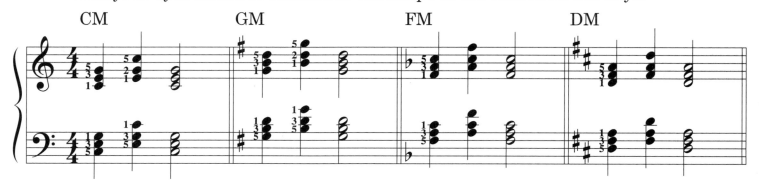

How many keys can you play in? Cross each one out as you play it.
C, Cm, G, Gm, D, Dm, A, Am, E, Em, B, Bm, F♯, F♯m, C♯, C♯m.

FJH2075

Before playing:

- Circle the **four** 1st inversion triads.

Bubbling Fountain

by Helen Marlais

Transpose to: D Major _____

A Major _____

F Major _____

Key of your choice: _____

After playing, ask yourself:
- Did I play with a *leggero* touch and sound?
- Did I pay attention to the dynamics?

* See dictionary on pp. 62-63.

Before playing:

- Find and play the 1st inversion triads.
  Notice the sequence in the R.H. at the beginning.

Waltz for a Windy Wednesday

by Kevin Olson

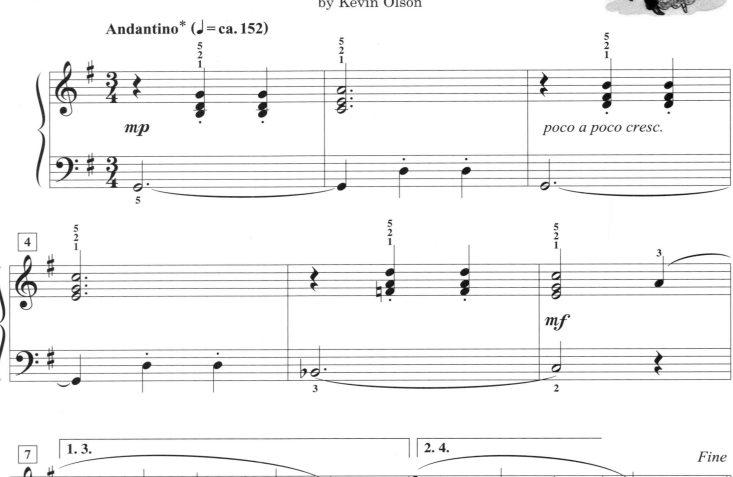

* See dictionary on pp. 62-63.

FJH2075

D.C. al Fine
(take repeat)

Sharp Key Signatures

This is the order of ♯'s
(read from left to right)

Father **C**harles **G**oes **D**own
And **E**nds **B**attle

Flat Key Signatures

This is the order of ♭'s
(read from left to right)

Battle **E**nds **A**nd **D**own
Goes **C**harles' **F**ather

Read aloud and play these on the piano:

1. Play the F♯. Go **up** a half step. You are on G. That is the name of the key—G Major.

2. Play the **last sharp** and go **up** a half step. You are on D. That is the name of the key— D Major.

3. Play the **last sharp** and go **up** a half step. You are on A. That is the name of the key— A Major.

4. Play the **last sharp** again. What key are you in? _____ Major.

5. Play the **last sharp** again. What key are you in? _____ Major.

1. Play the next-to-the-last flat. That is the name of the key— B♭ Major.

2. Play the next-to-the-last flat. That is the name of the key— E♭ Major.

3. Play the next-to-the-last flat. That is the name of the key— A♭ Major.

4. Play the next-to-the-last flat. That is the name of the key— D♭ Major.

5. Play the next-to-the-last flat. What is the name of the key? _____ Major.

- Continue through the keys. You'll practice writing these key signatures in the *Theory and Activity Book.*

FJH2075

Technique with Mozart
Review of Two-Octave Major Scales

CD 7 • MIDI 4

- C, G, D, A, E Major have the same fingering.
- Remember R.H. finger 3 and L.H. finger 3 always play at the same time.
- Remember which key your 4th finger plays. It will **only** be on this key.

C Major:

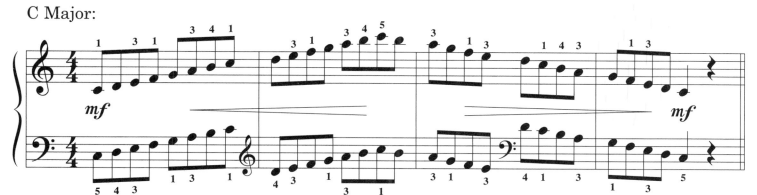

G Major:

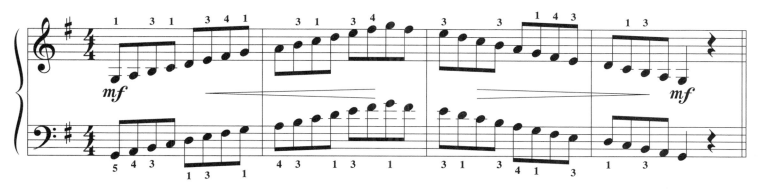

F Major: The thumbs of both hands play together (except to begin and end the scales.)
Notice which keys your 4th finger plays.

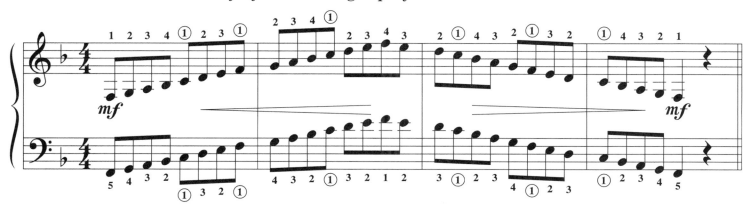

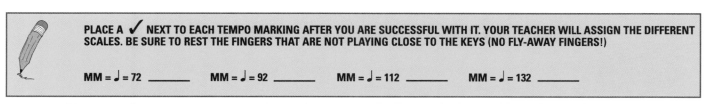

PLACE A ✔ NEXT TO EACH TEMPO MARKING AFTER YOU ARE SUCCESSFUL WITH IT. YOUR TEACHER WILL ASSIGN THE DIFFERENT SCALES. BE SURE TO REST THE FINGERS THAT ARE NOT PLAYING CLOSE TO THE KEYS (NO FLY-AWAY FINGERS!)

MM = ♩ = 72 _____   MM = ♩ = 92 _____   MM = ♩ = 112 _____   MM = ♩ = 132 _____

Play Your Scales and Chords Every Day™ Books 5 and 6 are a great way to learn all your scales and chords.

Before playing:

- Mark the ABA (ternary form) in the music.

When playing:

- Stay close to the keys and "kick off" from the keys with your wrist and forearm **together** as you play each triad.

The Masked Bandit

by Helen Marlais

Con moto (♩ = ca. 88)

* *sfz* (*sforzando*) means to play with a sudden, strong accent.

After playing, ask yourself:
- Did I feel my wrists and forearms kick off the keys with each *staccato* triad?

CD 10 • MIDI 6

Technique with Chopin
Review of 2nd inversion triads

Triads and Inversions

• Notice there are different ways to play a D Major triad:

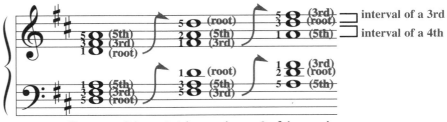

In 2nd inversion triads, the **root** is in the **MIDDLE** of the triad. The lower two notes form the interval of a 4th.

Chopin says:
Before playing each exercise, circle the 2nd inversion triads.

• Use a rebound *staccato* to spring off the keys.

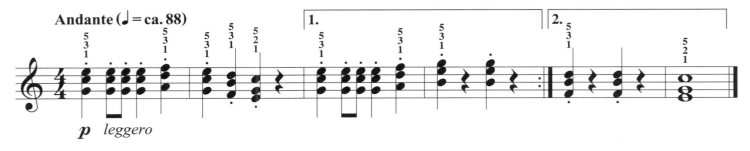

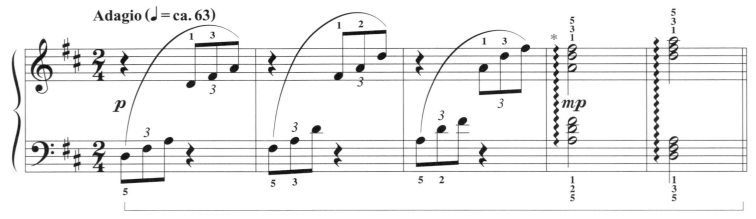

Key of: _____

* This sign means to roll the chord, bottom to top, one note at a time, like a harp.

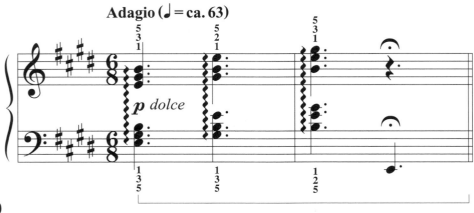

• Listen so that the top note of the R.H. triad is played **on** the beat.

FJH2075

Play first:

root position | 1st inversion | 2nd inversion

Before playing:

- Block every triad in the L.H., noticing which ones are in 2nd inversion.
- Play the melody, noticing the finger substitutions.

CD 11/12 • MIDI 7

The Old Church
by Helen Marlais

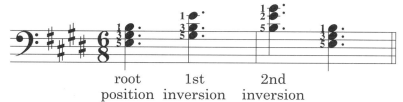

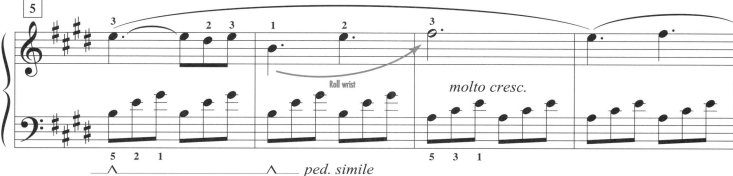

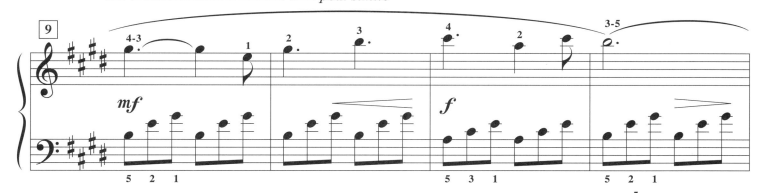

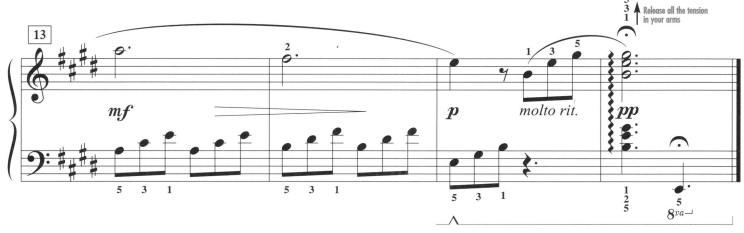

Before playing:

• Tap the rhythm hands together.

While learning:

• Practice this piece without the pedal until
  it is accurate. Then add the pedal.

Sloop John B

Bahamian Folk Song
Arranged by Edwin McLean

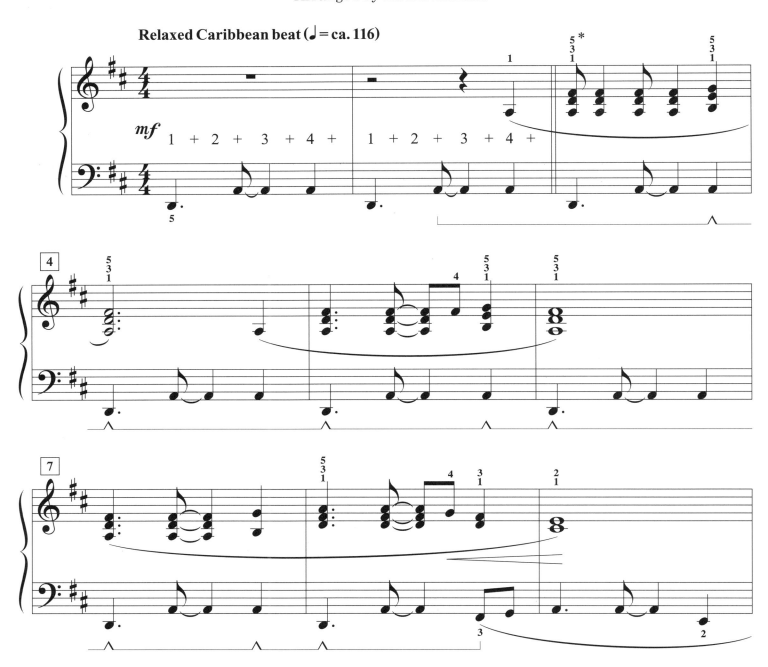

* You can use fingers "124" as well in measures 3, 4, 5, 6, and everywhere else there is a D Major
2nd inversion triad.

FJH2075

For supplementary repertoire, use *Succeeding with the Masters®, Volume 1; The Festival Collection®, Book 3; Etudes with Technique, Book 3;* and *In Recital®, Book 4.*

Before playing:

- This piece is in AB form. This is also called BINARY FORM. Mark the form directly in your score.

CD 15/16 • MIDI 9

When playing:

- Release your forearm muscles immediately after you drop your arm weight to the bottom of the keys. Push off the keys with your wrists and forearms, (wrists first) lifting your arm weight out of the keys.

Theme and Variation

by Cornelius Gurlitt
1820-1901, Germany

Andantino (♩. = ca. 96)

* **Portato**

A *staccato* dot with a slur means to play halfway between *legato* and *staccato*. Think "sticky" when you play, listening for the space between each chord.

UNIT 3

Technique with Mozart
Review of Intervals (2nds through octaves)

- Melodic intervals are notes played one after the other, while harmonic intervals are notes played together to create harmony.

Mozart says: Play these intervals, using **arm rotation**.
"Throw" your arm from side to side for the 7th and the octave.

Major 2nd   Major 3rd   Perfect 4th   Perfect 5th   Major 6th   Major 7th   Perfect Octave

- Transpose to different keys.

Octave Exercise:

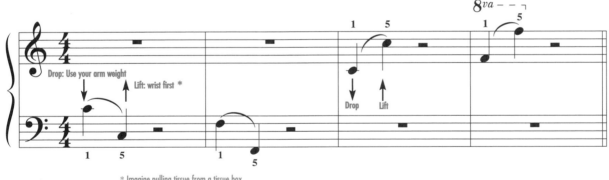

Drop: Use your arm weight

Lift: wrist first *

Drop   Lift

* Imagine pulling tissue from a tissue box
when you lift off, out of the key.

Motive:

- A rhythmic or melodic pattern that is short and easy to recognize is called a **motive**.
- A motive is often repeated during a piece.
- Practice the following motives and you'll be ready for the next piece.

motive repeated
and changed slightly

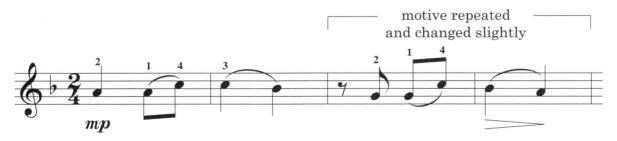

FJH2075

Before playing:

- Notice the opening motive in m.1 and 2. It is repeated and changed slightly in m. 3 and 4, 9 and 10. Where else do you see it?

Arioso

by Daniel Gottlob Türk
1750-1813, Germany

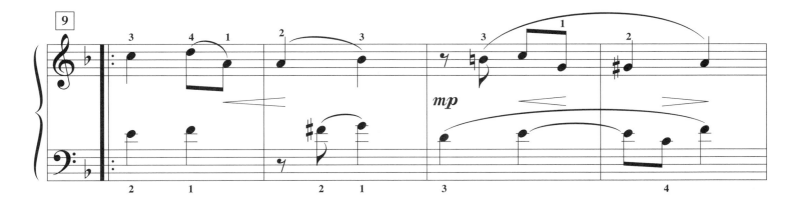

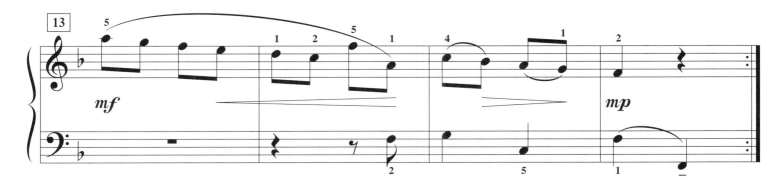

Ludwig van Beethoven (1770-1827) completed the Symphony No. 9 in D minor in 1824. It was premiered in Vienna, Austria. It is one of the most well-known works in all of Western classical repertoire. This work is called a "choral symphony." In the last movement, four soloists and large choir sing the words of "Ode to Joy" along with the orchestra. The words were written by Friedrich Schiller, a well-known German poet. Beethoven shared the stage with the conductor at the premiere, and when the audience applauded afterward, Beethoven was turned around so that he could face the audience to see them. He couldn't hear them because of his deafness. The audience gave him five standing ovations throughout the performance.

CD 20/21 • MIDI 12

Ode to Joy

(Theme from Symphony No. 9)
by Ludwig van Beethoven
1770-1827, Germany
Arranged by Timothy Brown

FJH2075

After playing, ask yourself:
- Did I bring out the important theme throughout the piece?

Technique with Beethoven
The Dominant Seventh (V⁷) Chord

- The dominant chord is built on the 5th note of the scale. It is a major triad.

The primary chords in C Major:

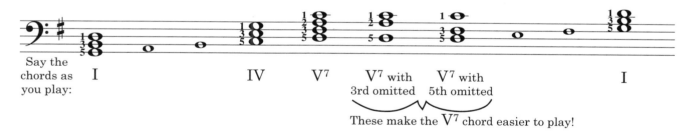

	I			IV	V⁷		I
	tonic			subdominant	dominant seventh		
	C			F	G⁷		

- The V^7 chord is a four-note chord. An interval of a minor 7th is added above the root.

Beethoven says: As you play each chord, drop your wrist and forearm, using arm weight. Notice your arm hanging freely from your shoulder joint.

The primary chords in G Major:

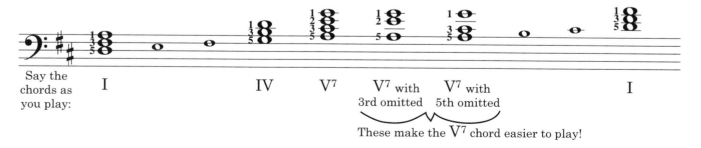

Say the chords as you play: I   IV   V⁷   V⁷ with 3rd omitted   V⁷ with 5th omitted   I

These make the V^7 chord easier to play!

The primary chords in D Major:

Say the chords as you play: I   IV   V⁷   V⁷ with 3rd omitted   V⁷ with 5th omitted   I

These make the V^7 chord easier to play!

FJH2075

When playing:

- Notice that the L.H. has a bass note (♩.) which is held while the inner notes of the harmony are played.

Carl Czerny (1791-1857) was born in Vienna, Austria. From the age of 10-13 he studied with Beethoven. He premiered Beethoven's Piano Concerto No. 5 when he was 21.

In the Swiss Alps

Carl Czerny
1791-1857, Austria

Before playing:

- Find and play the V⁷ chords in the L.H.
- Find and play the 1st and 2nd inversion triads.

Jumping on the Trampoline

by Kevin Costley

CD 25/26 • MIDI 15

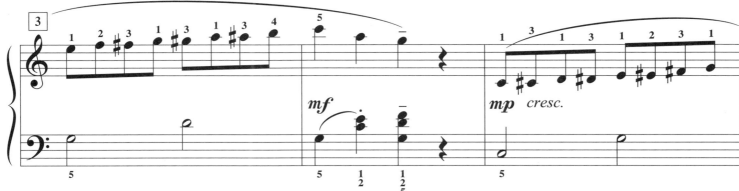

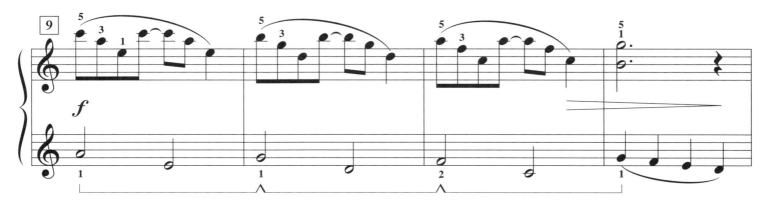

FJH2075

The Trill

-  or **tr** is a rapid alternation between two notes next to each other. In the Baroque era trills usually begin on the note **above** the principal (printed) note. Play the trill **on** the beat.

A Little Baroque*

by Mary Leaf

CD 27/28 • MIDI 16

FJH2075

* In the Theory Book you will learn more about the different eras and Baroque music.

CD 29 • MIDI 17

Technique with Haydn

1. The Key of E Minor
- As you know, every major scale has a **relative minor** scale that shares the same key signature. E minor is the relative minor of G Major. (Count **three** half steps down from G and you will find E.)

2. E natural minor scale
- Notice which key your 4th finger plays. Fingers "3" play at the same time. Practice hands alone, then hands together.

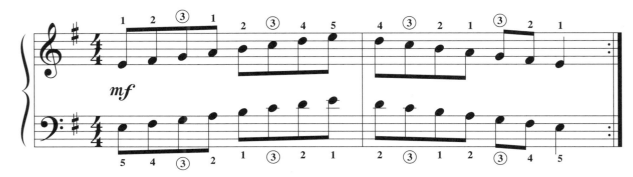

3. Harmonic minor form (raised 7th note ascending and descending)

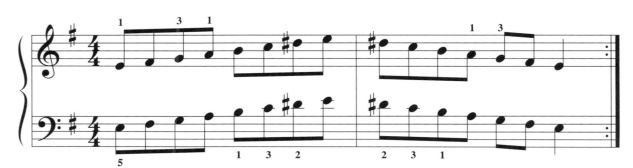

4. Melodic minor form (raised 6th and 7th notes ascending and lowered on descending)

Haydn says:
Play evenly and *legato* with flexible wrists. Play on the pads of your fingers and free your arms at the shoulder joints.

FJH2075

5. **Playing the i (tonic) and V⁷ (dominant 7th) chords**

CD 30 • MIDI 18

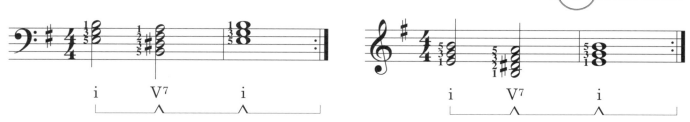

i   V⁷   i   i   V⁷   i

6. **Playing an E minor cadence**
 • Play as written, and then add the L.H. one octave below.

i   iv   i   V⁷   i

Haydn says:
Add pedal if
you like!

7. **Playing broken chords**

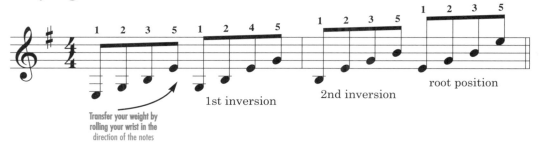

Transfer your weight by
rolling your wrist in the
direction of the notes

1st inversion   2nd inversion   root position

8. **Playing an arpeggio**
 • Practice hands apart, then hands together.

Drop arm weight   Drop wrist   Lift   Roll wrist to the left
Lift
Lift

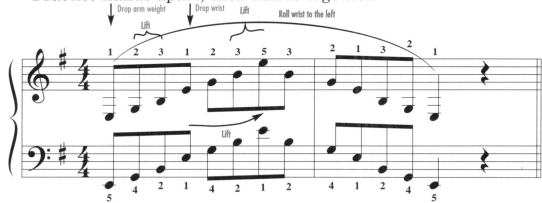

	PLACE A ✓ AFTER EACH TEMPO MARKING ONCE YOU ARE SUCCESSFUL WITH IT.						
	MONDAY	TUESDAY	WEDNESDAY	THURSDAY	FRIDAY	SATURDAY	SUNDAY
♩ = 72	_____	_____	_____	_____	_____	_____	_____
♩ = 96	_____	_____	_____	_____	_____	_____	_____
♩ = 126	_____	_____	_____	_____	_____	_____	_____
♩ = ___ YOUR CHOICE	_____	_____	_____	_____	_____	_____	_____

Before playing:

· Notice the motives throughout this piece.

Sakura

(Cherry Blossoms)

Japanese Folk Song
Arranged by Timothy Brown

Andante moderato (♩ = ca. 104)

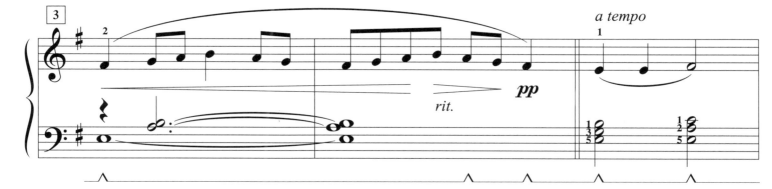

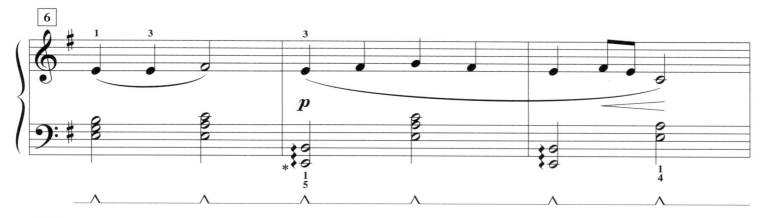

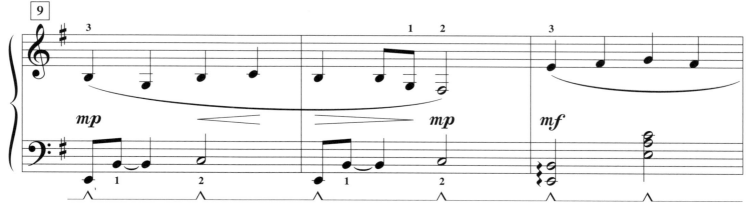

* The top of the rolled 5th (B) should be played exactly at the same time as the R.H. note.

FJH2075

* *Pianississimo* – quieter than ***pp***.

After playing, ask yourself:
· Did I shape every phrase beautifully?

Before playing:

- Listen to the CD and notice how the melody notes with the tenuto marks are emphasized.

She's Like the Swallow

Canadian Folk Song
Traditional
Arranged by Edwin McLean

FJH2075

UNIT 6

CD 35 • MIDI 21

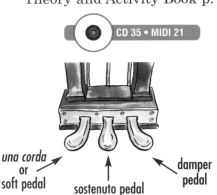

una corda
or
soft pedal → sostenuto pedal ← damper pedal

Technique with Chopin
Exploring Pedal Technique

- The damper pedal is used to sustain sound.
- It can also be used to add color.

- Mixing sounds by using the pedals is one of the most important ways to play artistically. You will learn about the soft pedal and the sostenuto pedals in Grade 5.

Chopin says:

Listen carefully when you change the pedal so that the different harmonies do not overlap. Your ear must always be your guide.

Mystical Waters
by Helen Marlais

Andante (♩ = ca. 69)

FJH2075

Circle of Fifths

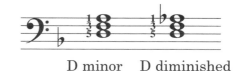

- It is important to know which key you are playing in.
- The "circle of fifths" is a great way to learn key signatures.
- Learn more about this in the *Theory and Activity Book*.

Technique with Mozart
Learning Diminished Triads

 Mozart says:
To build a diminished (dim.) triad, lower the 5th note of a minor triad. The sound has a "wandering" quality.

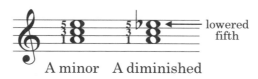

A minor   A diminished   D minor   D diminished

- Play the following triads using the two tempo markings below. Once you begin, continue in the circle of fifths.
  maestoso (with majesty) ♩ = 69   *spiritoso* (with spirit) ♩ = 96

- Drop your arm weight to the bottom of the keys. Then slowly push off the keys with your wrists and forearms, lifting your arm weight out of the keys.

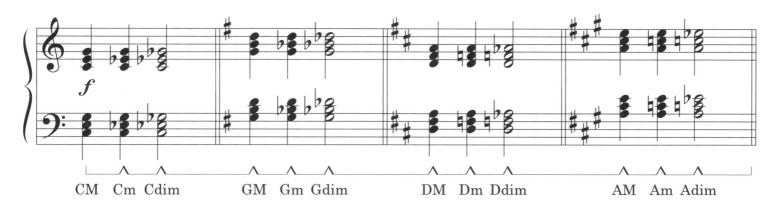

CM Cm Cdim   GM Gm Gdim   DM Dm Ddim   AM Am Adim

Cont.: E, B, F♯, C♯ ...

> - Practice these triads while you learn all of Grade 4.
> - You will be ready to play pieces with these in Grade 5.

FJH2075

While playing:

- Listen to your pedaling carefully. For some
  measures, pedal on the downbeats. Other
  measures will sound better pedaling more often
  or not at all!

 **CD 37/38 • MIDI 23**

Peace Like a River

Traditional American Spiritual
Arranged by Kevin Olson

Flowing (♩ = ca. 112)

Lyrics under the staves:

I've got peace like a riv - er, I've got peace like a

riv - er, I've got peace like a riv - er in my

soul; I've got peace like a riv - er, I've got

peace like a riv - er, I've got peace like a riv - er in my

FJH2075

Technique with Brahms

CD 39 • MIDI 24

1. **The Key of B♭ Major**
  • As in every major scale, the two half steps are between notes 3 and 4,
    and 7 and 8.

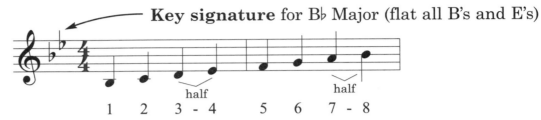

Key signature for B♭ Major (flat all B's and E's)

Brahms says:
Notice the fingering for the L.H. scale, and then the R.H. scale below.

2. **Playing the B♭ Major Scale**

What is the only key your **4th** finger plays? _____

What is the only key your **4th** finger plays? _____

In the R.H., your 4th finger begins and ends on B♭. For ease of playing, you may find it
more comfortable to begin and end with your 3rd finger. Then make a habit of it!

3. **The primary chords in B♭ Major**

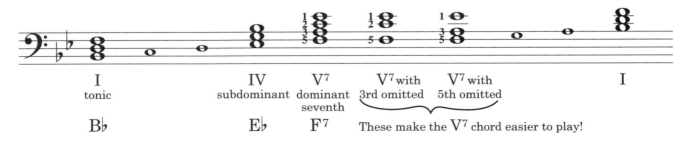

36

4. Playing a B♭ Major cadence

• Play as written, and then add the R.H. one octave higher.

I   IV   I   V⁷   I

Add pedal if you like!

5. Playing triads and inversions

• Practice hands apart, then hands together.

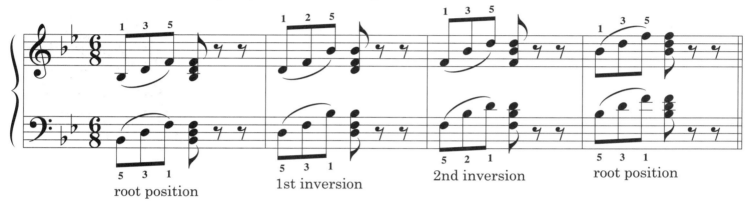

root position   1st inversion   2nd inversion   root position

6. Playing an arpeggio

• Practice hands apart, then hands together.

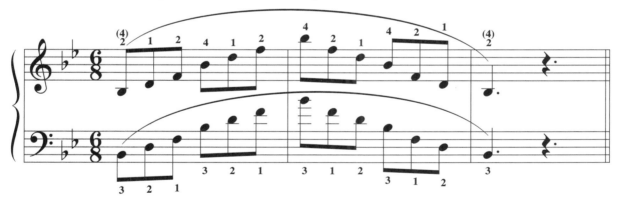

PLACE A ✓ BY EACH TEMPO MARKING AFTER YOU ARE SUCCESSFUL WITH THESE TWO PAGES. BE SURE TO REST THE FINGERS THAT ARE NOT PLAYING CLOSE TO THE KEYS (NO FLY-AWAY FINGERS!)

	MONDAY	TUESDAY	WEDNESDAY	THURSDAY	FRIDAY	SATURDAY	SUNDAY
♩ = 72	___	___	___	___	___	___	___
♩ = 96	___	___	___	___	___	___	___
♩ = 126	___	___	___	___	___	___	___
♩ = ___ YOUR CHOICE	___	___	___	___	___	___	___

 *Franz Liszt (1811-1886) is one of the greatest pianists to have ever lived. He was a wonderful composer, teacher, and conductor. He was also a benefactor of other composers, helping their music to become known throughout Europe. He was from Hungary and he wrote 19 Hungarian Rhapsodies. He was so well loved by audiences for his virtuosity that he reached the equivalent of "rock star" status in the 19th century. This piece was composed in 1847 and was so popular that Liszt wrote a version for orchestra soon after.*

Before playing:

- Block the L.H. notes in each measure to form a chord. When you practice them, say the names of the chords (V^7, I).

- Then practice the R.H., listening to the articulations. Notice the accents on many of the 3rd beats.

Theme from
Hungarian Rhapsody No. 2

by Franz Liszt
1811-1886, Hungary
Arranged by Timothy Brown

Vivace* ($\downarrow$ = 108 or faster)

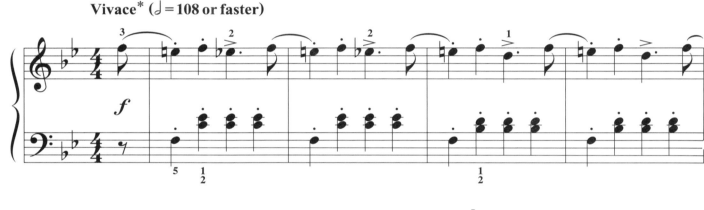

* See dictionary on p. 62-63.

FJH2075

* Play the small notes as grace notes ♪, quickly before the beat.

After playing, ask yourself:
- Did I play with excellent rhythm?

Technique with Beethoven

1. **The Key of G Minor**
   - G minor is the relative minor of B♭ Major.
     (They are three half steps away from each other.)
   - Like B♭ Major, G minor has 2 flats (B♭ and E♭.)

2. **G natural minor scale**
   - Which note does your 4th finger play in the R.H.?_____ in the L.H.?_____
   - Practice hands alone, then hands together.

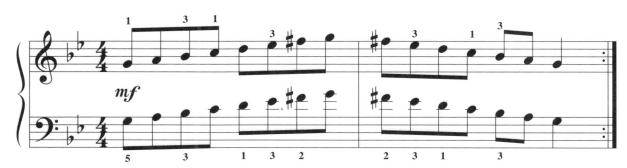

3. **Harmonic minor form** (raised 7th note ascending and descending)

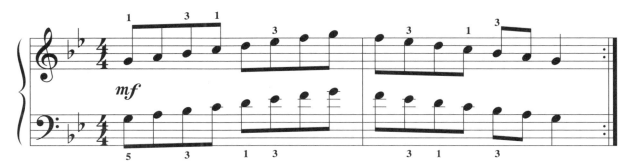

4. **Melodic minor form** (raised 6th and 7th notes ascending and lowered on descending)

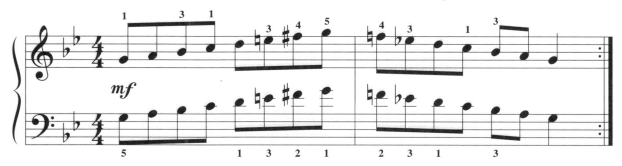

Beethoven asks:
Can you play these scales as two-octave scales?
After you can play two-octave scales, practice three-octaves scales in ♩♩♩ patterns.
Practice in triplets only when completely secure with two-octave scales.

FJH2075

5. **Playing the primary chords in G minor**
   • Play as written, and then add the R.H. one octave higher.

i	iv	V⁷	i
G minor	C minor	D⁷	G minor

6. **Playing a G minor cadence**

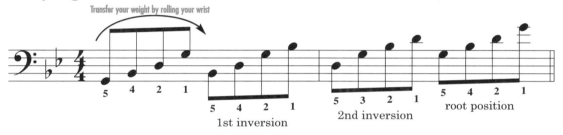

pesante (heavily)

Add pedal if you like!

Beethoven says: Say the names of the chords as you play!

7. **Playing broken chords**

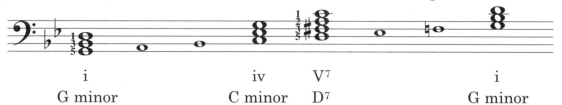

Transfer your weight by rolling your wrist

5 4 2 1

5 4 2 1
1st inversion

5 3 2 1
2nd inversion

5 4 2 1
root position

8. **Two-octave arpeggios**

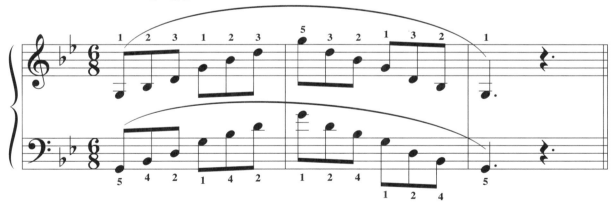

• **Parallel keys** share the same tonic note. For example, you can practice these exercises in G Major and then in G minor, and you will be playing in parallel keys.

	PLACE A ✔ NEXT TO EACH TEMPO MARKING AFTER YOU ARE SUCCESSFUL WITH THESE TWO PAGES.						
	MONDAY	TUESDAY	WEDNESDAY	THURSDAY	FRIDAY	SATURDAY	SUNDAY
♩ = 72	_____	_____	_____	_____	_____	_____	_____
♩ = 96	_____	_____	_____	_____	_____	_____	_____
♩ = YOUR CHOICE	_____	_____	_____	_____	_____	_____	_____

Before playing:

- Look at the last note of the piece. What is it? _____
  What key are you in? _____

When Johnny Comes Marching Home

Traditional American Folk Song
Arranged by Kevin Olson

FJH2075

Sixteenth Notes (16th notes)

CD 47 • MIDI 30

In $\frac{2}{4}$, $\frac{3}{4}$, and $\frac{4}{4}$, a ♩ = 1 beat.

The sixteenth note ♬ and the sixteenth rest ♰ receive a quarter (1/4) of a beat.

- Two sixteenth notes beamed together: ♫ = ♪

- Four sixteenth notes beamed together: ♬♬ = ♩

It's easy to count sixteenth notes. Clap and count aloud, accenting every downbeat: (♪ = 116, MM = ♪ = 104)

$\frac{3}{4}$ 1 e + a 2 e + a 3 e + a | 1 e + a 2 e + a 3 e + a :||

On the repeat, switch parts! Make a ———< to the ♩ This will give your playing forward direction.

Technique with Mozart

Use arm rotation

1. $\frac{3}{4}$

mp ———— *mf*   *mp* ———— *mf*

Transfer your weight by rolling your wrist in the direction of the notes.

↑ Push off!

mp ———— *mf*

2.

Use a rolling R.H. wrist

mf ↑ Kick off, wrist and forearm together

	PLACE A ✓ UNDER EACH DAY YOU PRACTICE THESE EXCERSISES. TRANSPOSE TO DIFFERENT KEYS IF YOU LIKE.						
	MONDAY	TUESDAY	WEDNESDAY	THURSDAY	FRIDAY	SATURDAY	SUNDAY
MM = ♪ = 72	_____	_____	_____	_____	_____	_____	_____
MM = ♩ = 56	_____	_____	_____	_____	_____	_____	_____
MM = ♩ = 80	_____	_____	_____	_____	_____	_____	_____

FJH2075

Before playing:

- Count and tap hands together.
- Find and play the two diminished triads in m.11–12.

Music for a Silent Movie
by Kevin Olson

When playing:

- Practice at a slow, "thinking" tempo
  (with the metronome) until you are sure of
  the correct rhythm, notes, fingering, and
  articulations.

Beethoven's Lost Penny

based on *Rage Over a Lost Penny* by Beethoven
by Timothy Brown

FJH2075

More Sixteenth Note Rhythm Patterns ♫♪ ♪♫

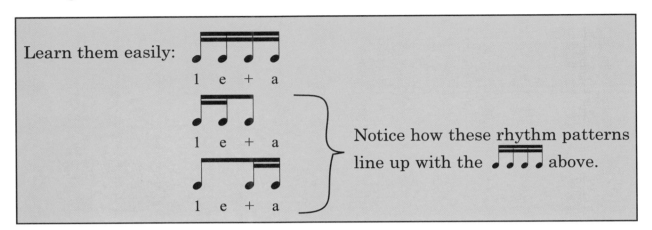

Learn them easily:

1 e + a

1 e + a

Notice how these rhythm patterns line up with the ♪♪♪♪ above.

1 e + a

♫♪ Here the ♪ replaces the **last** two ♪♪ in the group of four ♪♪♪♪

♪♫ Here the ♪ replaces the **first** two ♪♪ in the group of four ♪♪♪♪

1. It's easy to count these patterns. Clap and say aloud:

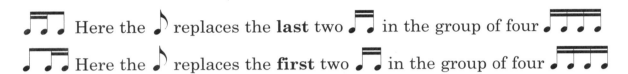

Here we go! To the show! What a blast!
1 e + a 2 e + a 3 e + a

Helpful Hint:

Make a ◁ to every ♩ when you count and clap. This will give your pieces forward direction.

I like to eat! I like to walk! I like to sleep!
1 e + a 2 e + a 1 e + a 2 e + a 1 e + a 2 e + a

2. Clap the following patterns with your teacher, counting aloud.

(♪=152, ♪=84, ♪=104)

1 e + a 2 e + a 3 e + a 4 e + a 1 e + a 2 e + a 3 e + a 4 e + a

1 e + a 2 e + a 3 e + a 1 e + a 2 e + a 3 e + a

FJH2075

Technique with Haydn

CD 52 • MIDI 33

Memorize the exercises below so you can listen and watch your fingers, hands, and arms as you play.

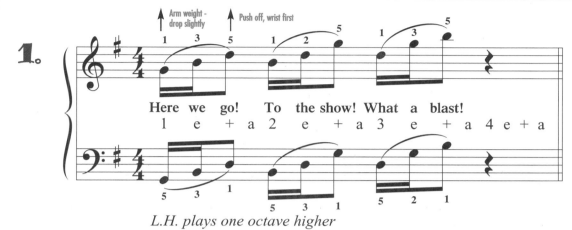

1.

Arm weight - drop slightly   Push off, wrist first

Here we go! To the show! What a blast!
1 e + a 2 e + a 3 e + a 4 e + a

L.H. plays one octave higher

2.

I like to eat!
1 e + a 2 e + a

I like to walk!

I like to sleep!

L.H. plays one octave higher

3.

1 e + a 2 e + a

Haydn says: Practice scale #3 as well as scale #4 hands together.

4.

1 e + a 2 e + a

Technique Tip: Transfer the weight of your arm to the right when ascending, and to the left when descending. Be careful not to twist or turn your wrist. Imagine a string pulling your elbow and forearm to the right and to the left.

PLACE A ✓ UNDER EACH DAY YOU PRACTICE THESE EXERCISES. TRANSPOSE THEM TO DIFFERENT KEYS.

MONDAY	TUESDAY	WEDNESDAY	THURSDAY	FRIDAY	SATURDAY	SUNDAY
___	___	___	___	___	___	___

Edvard Grieg wrote this piece as part of a play called Peer Gynt. It was first performed in 1876. In the Hall of the Mountain King are trolls, gnomes, goblins, children, and the king's relatives. Grieg (1843-1907) was a composer from Norway, and the folklore of this country is clearly evoked in this music.

Before playing:

- Notice the recurring motives. Then practice all of the moves.

When playing:

- Practice at a slow, "thinking" tempo, hands together.

In the Hall of the Mountain King

(from *Peer Gynt Suite*)
by Edvard Grieg
1843-1907, Norway
Arranged by Timothy Brown

CD 53/54 • MIDI 34

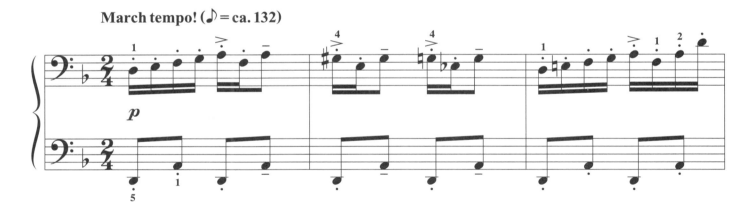

FJH2075

After playing, ask yourself:
- What is the mood of this piece?

_____ (you write)

Before playing:

· A **nocturne** is a piece about the night.
  See the dictionary on p.62 to learn more.

CD 55/56 • MIDI 35

Nocturne
by Timothy Brown

Cantabile (♩ = ca. 76)

Shift your weight by rolling your wrist to the right

cresc.

FJH2075

* *rallentando* means "becoming slower."

This work, the Prelude in C Major, is a fine example of a piece written in the Baroque Era, which lasted from around 1600 to 1750. This piece was written by one of the greatest composers of all time, Johann Sebastian Bach (1685-1750). He lived and worked his entire life in Germany. You will learn more about him in the Theory Book.

Prelude in C Major

BWV 846

by Johann Sebastian Bach, 1685-1750, Germany

Espressivo (♩ = ca. 69)

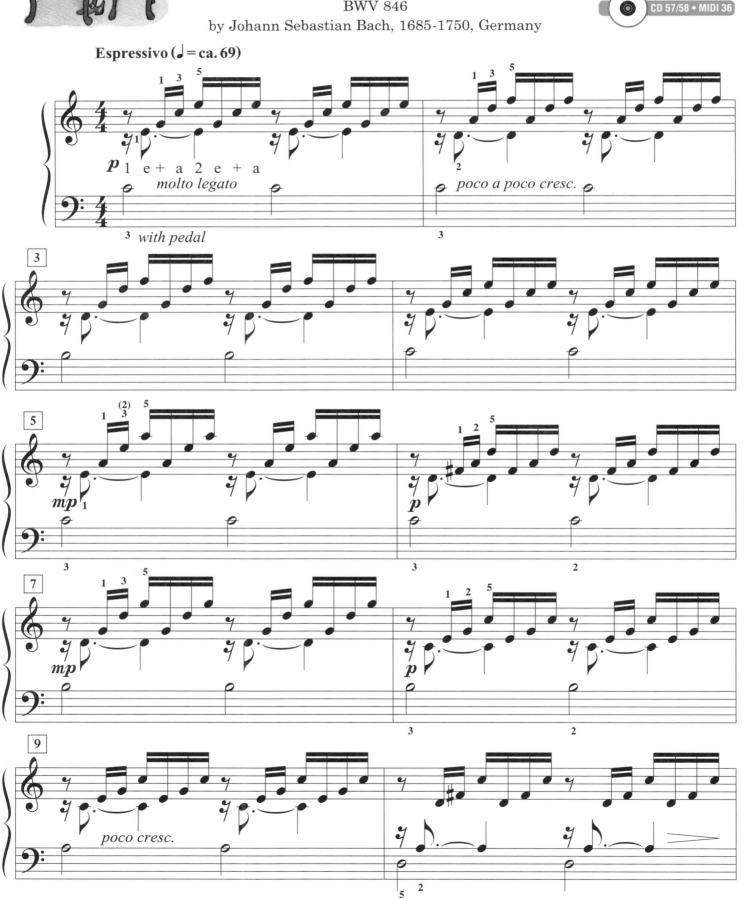

FJH2075

FJH2066

Dotted Eighth Note ♪. ♫

Before playing:

· Tap the rhythm of this piece hands together.

· Find and play the triads and inversions.

Clap and
count
aloud:

1 e + a

1 e + a

Theme from *The Marriage of Figaro*

by Wolfgang Amadeus Mozart

1756-1791, Austria

Arranged by Helen Marlais

CD 59/60 • MIDI 37

Hungarian Dance No. 5

by Johannes Brahms
1833-1897, Germany
Arranged by Timothy Brown

FJH2075

Sixteenth Notes in $\frac{3}{8}$ and $\frac{6}{8}$

Each ♩ = 1 beat; Each ♪ = 1/2 a beat.

Before playing:

- Tap the rhythm of the piece, hands together.
  Omit the grace note ♪ when first learning the piece.
  Add the ♪ when the notes and rhythm are secure.

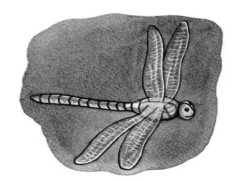

 CD 63/64 • MIDI 39

Dragonfly Etude*

by Hermann Berens
1826-1880, Sweden

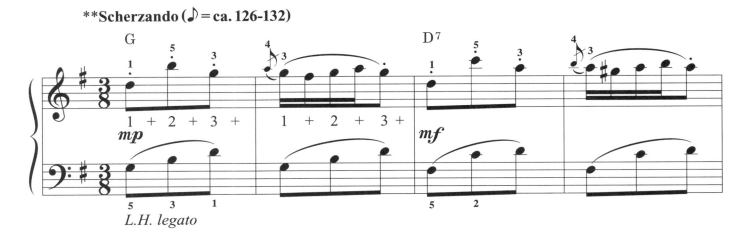

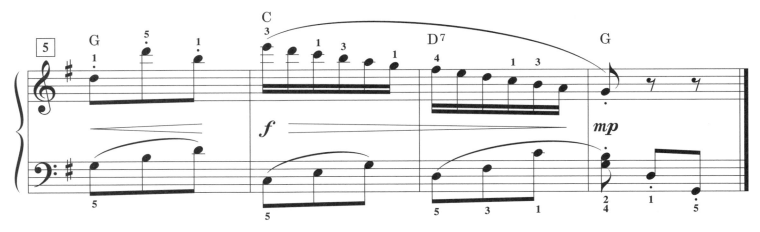

** *scherzando* - See dictionary on pp. 62-63.

After playing, ask yourself:
- Did the piece sound like the tempo suggests?

* An etude is a study focusing on a technical concept. What are you learning in this etude?

FJH2075

Before playing:

- Notice the rhythmic motives in this piece, such as ♫♩ and ♪ ♪ ♩·
- Find and practice the A minor scale in m.13-14, which form is it? _____
- Label the i and V triads in the first line.
- Is this piece in Binary (AB) or Ternary (ABA) form? _____
  Mark it in the score.

Magic Carpet Ride

by Ferdinand Beyer
1803-1863, Germany

Music Dictionary

Tempo Markings

largo - slow and dignified   *adagio* - slowly   *andante* - walking speed
andantino - a little faster than *andante*   *allegretto* - a little slower than *allegro*
moderato - moderate speed   *allegro* - happy, spirited   *spiritoso* - with spirit   *vivace* - very quickly

Music term	Definition	Found on page:
Arioso	a short vocal solo that is melodic and has the lyrical quality of an aria	17
arpeggio	when the notes of a triad or chord are played one after the other, instead of at the same time (blocked.) Pronounced: "ar-**peh**-joh"	27
binary form	when there are two sections to a piece (AB)	14
cantabile	(Italian, pronounced "kahn-TAH-bee-lay") In a singing manner	30
circle of fifths	shows the relationship between all 12 major and 12 minor keys through key signatures. Starting on any note, and moving up a fifth interval, one passes through all 12 keys to return to the starting note	33
con moto	(Italian, pronounced "kohn-MOH-toh") With motion	8
diminished triad	a minor triad with a lowered fifth. The fifth is lowered by one half step	33
dolce	(Italian, pronounced "DOHL-chay") Sweetly	10
dominant seventh chord	the dominant chord is built on the fifth note of the scale. It is a major triad. The V^7 chord is a four-note chord because an interval of a minor 7th is added above the root	20
espressivo	(Italian, pronounced "es-pres-SEE-voh") With expression	35
etude	a French word that means "a study." In these works, a performer focuses on a specific technique. Carl Czerny was one of the first to use the term and many composers followed such as Chopin, Liszt, Debussy, and Moszkowski	60
inversion	when the notes of a triad are moved around, or inverted, with the bottom note moving to the top position	2
key signature	the series of sharps or flats next to the time signature that shows what notes are altered in a piece. Key signatures are used to avoid the confusion of seeing many accidentals throughout a piece. Each major and minor key has a specific key signature. Once learned, key signatures become automatic	6
leggero	(Italian, pronounced "leh-JEHR-roh") Light, nimble	3
maestoso	(Italian, pronounced "mah-es-TOH-soh") With majesty	33

FJH2075

Certificate of Achievement

_____

Student

has completed

Helen Marlais'
Succeeding at the Piano®

Lesson and Technique Book
GRADE 4

You are now ready for
GRADE 5

_____   _____

Date   Teacher's Signature

T H E
F·J·H
MUSIC
COMPANY
I N C.

Frank J. Hackinson